The Centennial Meditation Of Columbia: A Cantata For The Inaugural Ceremonies At Philadelphia, May 10, 1876...

Dudley Buck, Sidney Lanier

Nabu Public Domain Reprints:

You are holding a reproduction of an original work published before 1923 that is in the public domain in the United States of America, and possibly other countries. You may freely copy and distribute this work as no entity (individual or corporate) has a copyright on the body of the work. This book may contain prior copyright references, and library stamps (as most of these works were scanned from library copies). These have been scanned and retained as part of the historical artifact.

This book may have occasional imperfections such as missing or blurred pages, poor pictures, errant marks, etc. that were either part of the original artifact, or were introduced by the scanning process. We believe this work is culturally important, and despite the imperfections, have elected to bring it back into print as part of our continuing commitment to the preservation of printed works worldwide. We appreciate your understanding of the imperfections in the preservation process, and hope you enjoy this valuable book.

1776—1876.
BY APPOINTMENT OF THE U. S. CENTENNIAL COMMISSION.

THE

CENTENNIAL

MEDITATION OF COLUMBIA.

A CANTATA

FOR

THE INAUGURAL CEREMONIES

AT

PHILADELPHIA, MAY 10, 1876.

POEM BY
SIDNEY LANIER,
OF GEORGIA.

MUSIC BY
DUDLEY BUCK,
OF CONNECTICUT.

NEW YORK:
G. SCHIRMER, 701 BROADWAY.

Copyright, 1876, by G. Schirmer.

Electrotyped by Smith & McDougal, 82 Beekman Street, New York.

THE CENTENNIAL MEDITATION OF COLUMBIA.

From this hundred-terraced height
Sight more large with nobler light
Ranges down yon towering years:
Humbler smiles and lordlier tears
  Shine and fall, shine and fall,
While old voices rise and call
Yonder where the to-and-fro
Weltering of my Long-Ago
Moves about the moveless base
Far below my resting-place.

Mayflower, Mayflower, slowly hither flying,
Trembling Westward o'er yon balking sea,
Hearts within *Farewell dear England* sighing,
Winds without *But dear in vain* replying,
Gray-lipp'd waves about thee shouted, crying
  No! It shall not be!

  Jamestown, out of thee—
  Plymouth, thee—thee, Albany—
  Winter cries, *Ye freeze: away!*
  Fever cries, *Ye burn: away!*
  Hunger cries, *Ye starve: away!*
  Vengeance cries, *Your graves shall stay!*

Then old Shapes and Masks of Things,
Framed like Faiths or clothed like Kings—
Ghosts of Goods once fleshed and fair,
Grown foul Bads in alien air—
War, and his most noisy lords,
Tongued with lithe and poisoned swords—

4

Error, Terror, Rage and Crime,
All in a windy night of time
Cried to me from land and sea,
No! Thou shalt not be!

Hark!
Huguenots whispering *yea* in the dark,
Puritans answering *yea* in the dark!
Yea, like an arrow shot true to his mark,
Darts through the tyrannous heart of Denial.
Patience and Labor and solemn-souled Trial,
Foiled, still beginning,
Soiled, but not sinning,
Toil through the stertorous death of the Night,
Toil, when wild brother-wars new-dark the Light,
Toil, and forgive, and kiss o'er, and replight.

Now Praise to God's oft-granted grace,
Now Praise to Man's undaunted face,
Despite the land, despite the sea,
I was: I am: and I shall be—
How long, Good Angel, O how long?
Sing me from Heaven a man's own song!

"Long as thine Art shall love true love,
Long as thy Science truth shall know,
Long as thine Eagle harms no Dove,
Long as thy Law by law shall grow,
Long as thy God is God above,
Thy brother every man below,
So long, dear Land of all my love,
Thy name shall shine, thy fame shall glow!"

O Music, from this height of time my Word unfold:
In thy large signals all men's hearts Man's Heart behold:
Mid-heaven unroll thy chords as friendly flags unfurled,
And wave the world's best lover's welcome to the world.

SIDNEY LANIER.

CENTENNIAL CANTATA.

Poem by SYDNEY LANIER.* Music by DUDLEY BUCK.*

* By appointment of the U. S. Centennial Commission.

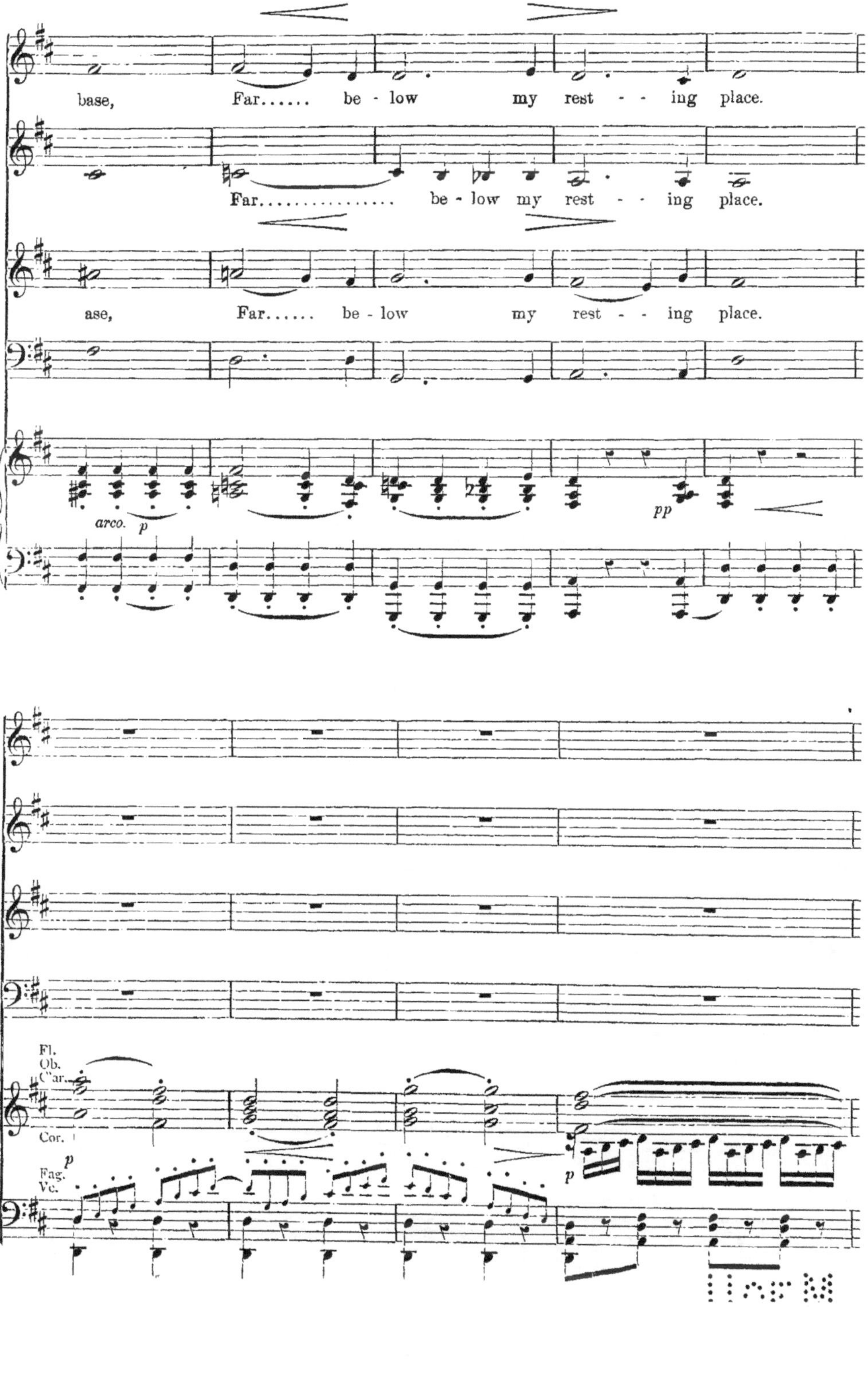
base, Far...... be - low my rest - - ing place.
Far................ be - low my rest - - ing place.
ase, Far...... be - low my rest - - ing place.
arco. p
pp
Fl.
Ob.
Clar.
Cor.
p
Fag.
Vc.
p

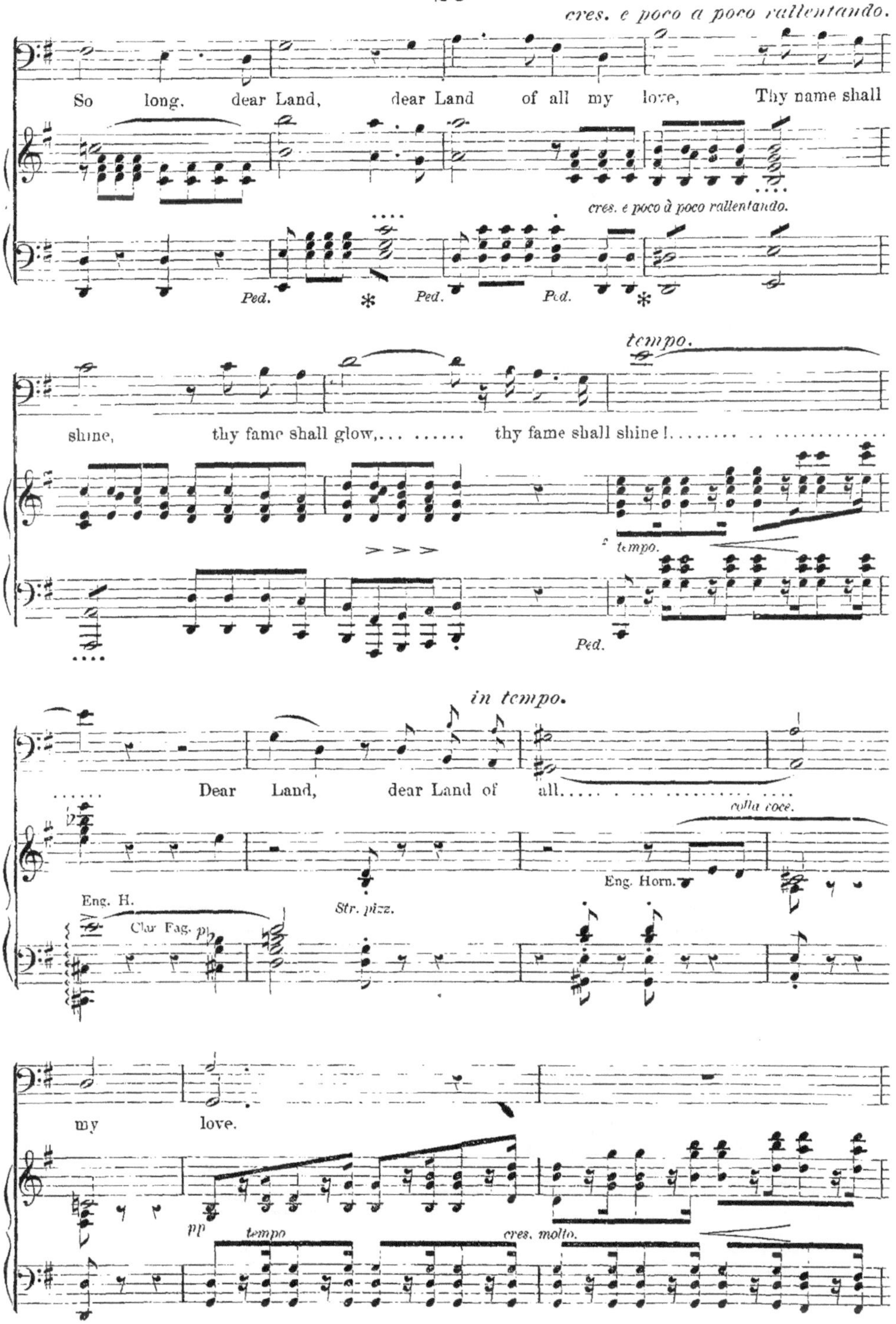
cres. e poco a poco rallentando.
So long. dear Land, dear Land of all my love, Thy name shall
cres. e poco à poco rallentando.
Ped.
shine, thy fame shall glow,... ...... thy fame shall shine!.......
tempo.
Ped.
in tempo.
...... Dear Land, dear Land of all.....
colla voce.
Eng. H.
Clar Fag.
Str. pizz.
Eng. Horn.
my love.
pp
tempo
cres. molto.